GLOUCESTERSHIRE

Wit & Humour

ROSIE DEAN

BRADWELL
BOOKS

Published by Bradwell Books

9 Orgreave Close Sheffield S13 9NP

Email: books@bradwellbooks.co.uk

Compiled by Rosie Dean

British Library Cataloguing in Publication Data: a catalogue record for this book is available from the British Library.

1st Edition

ISBN: 9781910551059

Print: Gomer Press, Llandysul, Ceredigion SA44 4JL

Design by: jenksdesign@yahoo.co.uk/07506 471162

Illustrations: ©Tim O'Brien 2014

At a cricket match in Stonehouse, a fast bowler sent one down and it just clipped the bail. As nobody yelled "Ow's att", the batsman picked up the bail and replaced it. He looked at the umpire and said, "Windy today int it?"

"Yes," said the umpire, "Mind it doesn't blow your cap off when you're walking back to the pavilion."

A Herefordshire man is driving through Gloucestershire, when he passes a farmer standing in the middle of a huge field. He pulls the car over and watches the farmer standing stock-still, doing absolutely nothing. Intrigued, the man walks over to the farmer and asks him, "Excuse me sir, but what are you doing?"

The farmer replies, "I'm trying to win a Nobel Prize."
"How?" Asks the puzzled Herefordshire man.

"Well," says the farmer, "I heard they give the prize to people who are outstanding in their field."

At a primary school in Stroud, the teacher came up with a good problem for her maths class to solve.

"Suppose, there were a dozen sheep and six of them jumped over a fence," she said to the group of seven-year-olds, "How many would be left?"

Little Harry, a farmer's son, put his hand up. "None," he answered. "None?" exclaimed his teacher. "Harry, I'm afraid you don't know your arithmetic."

"Really, Miss?" said Harry, cockily, "And you don't know your sheep. When one goes, they all go!"

A man walks into a pub in Amberley with a pork pie on his head.

The barman asks, "`ow bist? Why are you wearing a pork pie on yer head?"

The man replies, "It's a family tradition. We always wear pork pies on our heads on Tuesday."

The barman says, "But it's Wednesday."

Sheepishly, the man says, "Man, I must look like a real fool."

A gang of robbers broke into the Cheltenham Lawyers' Club by mistake. The old legal lions put up a fierce fight for their lives and their money. The gang was happy to escape in one piece. "It ain't so bad," one crook said. "At least we got fifty quid between us."

His boss screamed at him, "I warned you to stay clear of lawyers... we had £200 when we broke in!"

A Cirencester man went to his G.P. the other day and said, "Doctor, have you got anything for wind?"
"Sure," said the doctor and gave him a kite.

A man walks into the posh fishmongers in Nailsworth carrying a salmon under his arm. "Do you make fishcakes?' he asks.

"Of course," says the fishmonger.

"Oh good," says the man. "It's his birthday."

Q: What's black and white and very noisy?
A: A magpie with a drum kit.

Did you hear about the fight in the Indian restaurant in Gloucester? The chef was left in a korma.

Man: "I always carry a photo of my kids in my wallet.

Friend: "To remind you how lucky you are?"

Man: "No. To remind me why there's no money in there."

A Gloucester Spartans rugby prop: "Doctor, doctor, every morning when I get up and look in the mirror - I feel like throwing up. What's wrong with me?"

Doctor: "I don't know, but your eyesight is perfect."

Q: What do you call a ghost that likes curries?
A: A baltigiest

Alf and his old drinking buddy were in the pub in Nympsfield.

"I went to my son's for Sunday lunch," said Alf.

"Oh yeah," said his mate, "IT expert, int he?"

"Yeah," said Alf, "He's full of it. I asked if I could borrow a newspaper and he goes 'Dad, this is the 21st century. We don't waste money on newspapers in this house. You can borrow my new i-Pad.'" Alf took a sip of his pint. "Well, I can tell you, that bloody fly never knew what hit it..."

Q: Why did the Mushroom get invited to all the parties?
A: 'Coz he's a fungi!

A passenger in a taxi tapped the driver on the shoulder to ask him something.

The driver screamed, lost control of the cab, nearly hit a bus, drove up over the curb and stopped just inches from a large plate glass window.

For a few moments everything was silent in the cab, then the driver said, "Please, don't ever do that again. You scared the daylights out of me."

The passenger, who was also frightened, apologised and said he didn't realise that a tap on the shoulder could frighten him so much, to which the driver replied, "I'm sorry, it's really not your fault at all. Today is my first day driving a cab. I've been driving a hearse for the last twenty-five years."

It was match day for Gloucester City and excited Tigers fans filled the streets of Cheltenham, heading for stadium. A funeral procession drove slowly through the throng. One of the Gloucester City supporters stopped, took off his hat and bowed reverently as the hearse passed.

"That was a nice thing to do," remarked his mate.

"Well," said the Tigers fan, "She was a good wife to me for thirty odd years."

A plain Jane from Stroud goes to see Madame Grizelda, a fortune-teller, and asks about her future love life.

Madame Grizelda tells her, "Two men are madly in love with you – Mark and Maurice."

"Who will be the lucky one?" asks Jane excitedly.

Madame Grizelda answers, "Maurice will marry you, and Mark will be the lucky one."

Psychiatrist: "What's your problem?"
Patient: "I think I'm a chicken."
Psychiatrist: "How long has this been going on?"
Patient: "Ever since I was an egg!"

Two council workers on a site in Stroud are surveying land they're about to dig up.

The gaffer says to one of them, "You go and get the metal detector and check for pipe work and I'll get the kettle on and have a brew."

The gaffer gets the tea going while his mate starts work. Half-hour later the gaffer puts his paper down, next to his mug of tea, to find out how work is progressing and he finds his mate sitting on a wall scratching his head.

"What's up with you?" The gaffer asks. "There's pipework all over the place. Look!"

The young worker sets off across the land, the bleeper sounding continuously as the detector passes the ground in front of him.

The gaffer watches him, laughing, then he says, "Are you soft or what? You've got steel toe caps in your boots!"

"You're looking glum," the captain of Frocester C.C. remarked to one of his players.

"Yes, the doctor says I can't play cricket," said the downcast man.

"Really?" replied the captain, "I didn't know he'd ever seen you play?"

There's a man in Leominster who claims to have invented a game that's a bit like cricket; what he doesn't realise is Herefordshire County Cricket Club's been playing it for years.

A man from Thrupp decided to become a monk so he went to the monastery and talked to the head monk.

The head monk said, "You must take a vow of silence and can only say two words every three years."

The man agreed and after the first three years, the head monk came to him and said, "What are your two words?"

"Food cold!" the man replied.

Three more years went by and the head monk came to him and said, "What are your two words?"

"Robe dirty!" the man exclaimed.

Three more years went by and the head monk came to him and said, "What are your two words?"

"I quit!" said the man.

"Well," the head monk replied, "I'm not surprised. You've done nothing but complain ever since you got here!"

Q: Why did the piece of tofu cross the road?

A: To prove that it wasn't chicken.

A Brimscombe man fell out with his in-laws and banned them from entering the house while he was in it. His wife faithfully carried out his wishes until she was on her deathbed and then asked sadly, "Haven't I always been a supportive wife to you, John?"

"Yes, my dear," he replied, "The best."

"Then I would love it if you could grant my last request and let my sister Sarah ride in the first car with you at my funeral?"

"Alright, my dear," he agreed heavily, "But I'm warning you, it'll spoil all my pleasure!"

A man is up on a drunk and disorderly charge at Gloucester Magistrates Court. The magistrate, looking very weary, starts lecturing him: "You, sir, have been appearing before me constantly for the past twenty years..."

"That's correct, your honour," the man interrupts, "but I can't help it if you don't get promoted.

"Dad," says the little boy, "Can I play football with the lads in the street?"

"No," says his dad, "They swear too much."

"But you play with them, Dad?"

"I swear already."

A lad from Gloucester, who had just started his first term at Hereford Cathedral School, asked a prefect, "Can you tell me where the library's at?"

The older student said disdainfully, "At Hereford Cathedral School, we never end a sentence with a preposition." The new boy tried again, "Can you tell me where the library's at, you wally?"

Q: Why couldn't the lifeguard save the Stroud hippie swimming in the Severn Estuary?

A: Because he was too far out.

Down the King's Head, a group of blokes sit around drinking when a mobile phone on the table rings. One of the men picks up the mobile and puts the speaker-phone on.

A woman's voice says, "How are you, darling? I hope you don't mind but I've just seen a diamond ring priced £2000 and wondered if I can buy it? I've got your credit card with me."

"Of course, my dear, go ahead," answers the man.

"While I'm on," purrs the lady, "I've noticed a top of the range car I'd like. It's only £65,000, could I order that as well?"

"Of course, my angel," replies the man.

His friends around the table look at each other in disbelief as the lady continues, "And I've just noticed a house on the coast, lover. It's only £750,000 - could we have that as well please?"

"Of course, sugar," answers the man, without so much as blinking.

The phone call is ended and the man smiles at the others and takes a long swill of beer. Then he looks around and shouts "Anyone know whose phone this is?"

Derek and Duncan were long-time neighbours in Minchinhampton. Every time, Derek saw Duncan coming round to his house, his heart sank. This was because he knew that, as always, Duncan would be visiting him in order to borrow something and he was fed up with it.

"I'm not going to let Duncan get away with it this time," he said quietly to his wife, "Watch what I'm about to do."

"Hi there, I wondered if you were thinking about using your hedge trimmer this afternoon?" asked Duncan.

"Oh, I'm very sorry," said Derek, trying to look apologetic, "but I'm actually going to be using it all afternoon."

"In that case," replied Duncan with a big grin, "You won't be using your golf clubs, will you? Mind if I borrow them?"

The neighbour says, "Poor old grand-pa died this morning. He was out in the garden pulling up cabbages and he went, just like that – we think it was his heart."

"What a shame," commiserates the man next door, "What are you going to do now?"

"Open a tin of peas," says the neighbour.

Q: Why was the Blue-faced sheep arrested on the M5?

A: She did a ewe-turn

Two Highnam Court Cricket Club players are chatting in the bar after a match. "So did you have a hard time explaining last week's game to the wife?" says one.

"I certainly did," says the other, "She found out I wasn't there!"

Three Gloucestershire women are talking in a bar about a party they've been invited to.

The first one says, "We've got to all wear an item that matches something belonging to our husbands at this party, haven't we?"

"Yeah," said the other two, "But what?"

The first one continued, "Well, my husband's got black hair and I've got a little black dress I can diet into by then."

The second one says, "That's a good idea. My husband has got brown hair and I've got a brown dress I can diet into by then too."

The third one looks a bit hesitant and says, "I just need to go on a diet - my husband's bald!"

A lawyer at Gloucester Crown Court says to the judge, "Your Honour, I wish to appeal my client's case on the basis of newly discovered evidence."

His Lordship replies, "And what is the nature of the new evidence?"

The lawyer says, "My Lord, I discovered that my client still has £500 left."

Darren proudly drove his new convertible into Cirencester and parked it on the main street. He was on his way to the recycling centre to get rid of an unwanted gift, a foot spa, which he left on the back seat.

He had walked half way down the street when he realised that he had left the top down with the foot spa still in the back.

He ran all the way back to his car, but it was too late...another five foot spas had been dumped in the car.

Ten women out on a hen night in Gloucester thought it would be sensible if one of them stayed more sober than the other nine and looked after the money to pay for their drinks. After deciding who would hold the money, they all put twenty pounds into the kitty to cover expenses. At closing time after a few spritzers, several vodka and cokes, and a Pina Colada each, they stood around deciding how to divvy up the leftover cash.

"How do we stand?" said Sharon.

"Stand?!" said Debbie. "That's the easy part! I'm wondering how I can walk. I've missed the last bus to Quedgeley!"

A man rushed into Gloucestershire Royal Hospital and asked a nurse for a cure for hiccups. Grabbing a cup of water, the nurse quickly splashed it into the man's face.

"What did you that for?" screamed the man, wiping his face.

"Well, you don't have the hiccups now, do you?" said the nurse.

"No," replied the man. "But my wife out in the car does."

When the manager of Bristol Rovers started to tell the team about tactics, half the players thought he was talking about a new kind of peppermint.

One afternoon at University of Gloucester, a group of freshers, who had just started their psychology course, were attending one of their first seminars. The topic was emotional extremes.

"Let's begin by discussing some contrasts," said the tutor. He pointed to a student in the front row, "What is the opposite of joy?"

The student thought about it briefly, then answered "Sadness."

The tutor asked another student, "What is the opposite of depression?"

She paused then said, "Elation."

"And you," the tutor said to another student sitting at the back, "What about the opposite of woe?"

The student thought for a moment, then replied, "Um, I believe that would be 'giddy up'."

A police officer arrived at the scene of a major pile up on the M5.

The officer runs over to the front car and asks the driver, "Are you seriously hurt?"

The driver turns to the officer and says, "How the heck should I know? Do I look like a lawyer?"

Riding the favourite in the Cheltenham Gold Cup, the jockey is well ahead of the field. Suddenly he's hit on the head by a free-range turkey and a string of the field. Suddenly he's hit on the head by a free-range turkey and a string of sausages. He manages to keep control of his mount and pulls back into the lead, only to be struck by a box of Christmas crackers and a dozen mince pies as he goes over the last fence. With great skill he manages to steer the horse to the front of the field once more then, on the home straight, he's struck on the head by a bottle of sherry and a Christmas pudding. Thus distracted, he comes in second. He immediately goes to the stewards to complain that he has been seriously hampered.

One winter's night, a lorry is going along the road near Tewkesbury when the car behind, driving in from Herefordshire, starts flashing its headlights and sounding its horn. This goes on for a good ten minutes before the car finally overtakes the lorry on the A38 and as it does so the driver, who is from Ledbury, rolls the window down and shouts to the lorry driver, "Hey, you! Don't you realise you're losing your load off the back?"

"I blooming well hope so!" The lorry driver shouts back. "I'm gritting the roads, int I!?"

In a school in Chipping Sodbury, a little boy just wasn't getting good marks. One day, his teacher was checking his homework and said, "Lee, once again I'm afraid I can only give you two out of ten."

Little Lee looked up at her and said, "Well, Miss, I don't want to scare you, but…"

He stopped, a worried expression appeared on his face.

"What is it? Tell me, Lee," said his teacher kindly.

"Well," said the boy, "my daddy says if I don't get better marks soon, somebody is going to get a spanking."

Four students at the Royal Agricultural University in Cirencester were taking their degree and had done very well in their exams so far. Because of this, even though their last exam of the year was fast approaching, the four friends decided to go back to their hometown, Cheltenham, and catch up with some friends there. They had a great time partying.

However, after all the fun, they slept all day on Sunday and didn't make it back to Cirencester until early Monday morning which was the time of their final exam. Rather than taking the exam, they decided to find their professor after it was over and explain to him why they missed it. They told him that they had gone home to do some studying for the weekend and had planned to come back in time for the exam. But unfortunately, they had a flat tyre on the way back, didn't have a spare, and couldn't get help for a long time. As a result, they had only just arrived!

The professor thought it over and then agreed they could make up their final exam the following day. The four were very relieved. They studied hard that night - all night - and went in the next day at the time the professor had told them. He placed them in separate rooms and handed each of them a test booklet and told them to begin.

The first question was worth five points. It was something simple about a specific agricultural topic. "Great," they all thought, "This is going to be easy." They each finished the problem and turned the page. On the second page was written, "Question 2 (for 95 points): Which tyre?"

An old bloke at the bus stop outside Cheltenham General Hospital is talking to the next person in the queue whilst rubbing his head.

"My wooden leg int half giving me some gyp," complained the old boy.

The person in the queue looks at him, wondering why he keeps rubbing his head, and says, "Really? Why?"

The old man retorted, "Cos my missus keeps hitting me over the head with it!"

A policeman stops a man in a car in the middle of Gloucester with a fallow deer in the front seat.

"Evening, sir, what are you doing with that deer?" He asks. "You should take it to a zoo."

The following week, the same policeman sees the same man again with the fallow deer in the front seat of the car. Both of them are wearing sunglasses. The policeman pulls him over. "I thought you were going to take that deer to the zoo?"

The man replies, "I did. We had such a good time we are going to the beach at Weston-super-Mare this weekend!"

The president of the Cheltenham Vegetarian Society really couldn't control himself any more. He simply had to try some pork, just to see what it tasted like. So one day he told his members he was going away for a short break. He left town and headed to a restaurant in Tetbury. He sat down, ordered a roasted pig, and waited impatiently for his treat. After only a few minutes, he heard someone call his name, and, to his horror, he saw one of his members walking towards him. At exactly the same moment, the waiter arrived at his table, with a huge platter, holding a whole roasted pig with an apple in its mouth. "Isn't this place something?" said the president, thinking quickly, "Look at the way they serve apples!"

Sam worked in a telephone marketing company in Gloucester. One day he walked into his boss's office and said, "I'll be honest with you, I know the economy isn't great, but I have three companies after me, and, with respect, I would like to ask for a pay rise."

After a few minutes of haggling, his manager finally agreed to a 5% pay rise, and Sam happily got up to leave.

"By the way," asked the boss as Sam went to the door, "Which three companies are after you?"

"The electric company, the water company, and the phone company," Sam replied.

A farmer was driving along a country road near the village of Bishops Cleeve with a large load of fertiliser. A little boy, playing in front of his cottage, saw him and called out, "What do you have on your truck?"

"Fertiliser," the farmer replied"

What are you going to do with it?" asked the little boy."

Put it on strawberries," answered the farmer.

"You ought to live here," the little boy advised him. "We put sugar and cream on ours."

It was a quiet night in Bussage Chalford and a man and his wife were fast asleep, when there was an unexpected knock on the door. The man looked at his alarm clock. It was half past three in the morning. "I'm not getting out of bed at this time," he thought and rolled over.

There was another louder knock.

"Aren't you going to answer that?" asked his wife irritably.

So the man dragged himself out of bed and went downstairs. He opened the door to find a strange man standing outside. It didn't take the homeowner long to realise the man was drunk. "Hi there," slurred the stranger. "Can you give me a push?"

"No, I'm sorry I most certainly can't. It's half past three in the morning and I was in bed," said the man and he slammed the front door.

He went back up to bed and told his wife what happened. "That wasn't very nice of you," she said. "Remember that night we broke down in the pouring rain on the way to pick the kids up from the babysitter, and you had to knock on that man's door to get us started again? What would have happened if he'd told us to get lost?"

"But the man who just knocked on our door was totally pickled," replied her husband.

"Well, we can at least help move his car somewhere safe and sort him out a taxi," said his wife. "He needs our help."

So the husband got out of bed again, got dressed, and went downstairs. He opened the door, but couldn't to see the stranger anywhere so he shouted, "Hey, do you still want a push?"

In answer, he heard a voice call out, "Yes please!"

So, still unable to see the stranger, he shouted, "Where are you?"

"I'm over here, mate,"
the stranger
replied, "on your
swing."

A lady works in Gloucester and everyday she passes a pet shop. One day she sees a parrot in the window. She stops to admire the bird. The parrot says to her, "Alright, me lover…you're a right, rasty old scutler."

Well, the lady is furious! She storms off but, on her way back from work, she has to pass the pet shop and when the parrot sees her it says, "Alright, me lover… you're a right, rasty old scutler."

She is incredibly angry now so she goes to the manager and threatens to sue the pet shop and demands to have the bird put down. The manager apologises profusely and promises that the bird won't say it again. The next day, she decides to go back and check. She walks past the parrot and, when it sees her, it says, "Alright, me lover…"

The woman stops, scowls and with an icy stare, says, "Yes?"

The parrot struts back and forth on its perch in a cocky manner looking at her, then it says, "You know."

A pupil at a school in Stroud asked his teacher, "Are 'trousers' singular or plural?"

The teacher replied, "They're singular on top and plural on the bottom."

Phil's nephew came to him with a problem. "I have my choice of two women," he said, with a worried frown, "A beautiful, penniless young girl whom I love dearly, and a rich widow who I don't really love."

"Follow your heart," Phil counselled, "marry the girl you love."

"Very well, Uncle Phil," said the nephew, "That's sound advice. Thank you."

"You're welcome," replied Phil with a smile, "By the way, where does the widow live?"

A high-rise building was going up in Gloucester, and three steel erectors sat on a girder having their lunch.

"Oh, no, not cheese and pickle again," said Jim, the first one, "If I get the same again tomorrow, I'll jump off the girder.'

Horace opened his packet. "Oh, no, not a chicken salad with lettuce and mayo," he said. "If I get the same again tomorrow, I'll jump off too."

Andy, the third man, opened his lunch. "Oh, no, not another potato sandwich," he said. "If I get the same again tomorrow, I'll follow you two off the girder."

The next day, Jim got cheese and pickle. Without delay, he jumped. Horace saw he had chicken salad with lettuce and

mayo, and, with a wild cry, he leapt too. Then the third man, Andy, opened his lunchbox. "Oh, no," he said. "Potato sandwiches." And he too jumped.

The foreman, who had overheard their conversation, reported what had happened, and the funerals were held together.

"If only I'd known," sobbed Jim's wife.

"If only he'd said," wailed Horace's wife.

"I don't understand it at all," said Andy's wife. "He always got his own sandwiches ready."

A farmer from Herefordshire once visited a farmer based near Long Newnton. The visitor asked, "How big is your farm?" to which the Gloucestershire farmer replied, "Can you see those trees over there? That's the boundary of my farmland".

"Is that all?" said the Herefordshire farmer, "It takes me three days to drive to the boundary of my farm."

The Long Newnton man looked at him and said, "I had a car like that once."

The nervous young batsman playing for North Cerney C.C. was having a very bad day. In a quiet moment in the game, he muttered to the one of his team mates, "Well, I suppose you've seen worse players."

There was no response...so he said it again, "I said 'I guess you've seen worse players'."

His team mate looked at him and answered, "I heard you the first time. I was just trying to think..."

For a minute Bristol Rovers were in with a chance – then the game started.

One day at Gloucestershire Royal Hospital, a group of primary school children were being given a tour. A nurse showed them the x-ray machines and asked them if they had ever had broke a bone.

One little boy raised his hand, "I did!"

"Did it hurt?" the nurse asked.

"No!" he replied.

"Wow, you must be a very brave boy!" said the nurse. "What did you break?"

"My sister's arm!"

A woman from Stroud called Lizzie was still not married at thirty-five and she was getting really tired of going to family weddings especially because her old Aunt Maud always came over and said, "You're next!"

It made Lizzie so annoyed she racked her brains to figure out how to get Aunt Maud to stop. Sadly, an old uncle died and there was a big family funeral. Lizzie spotted Aunt Maud in the crematorium, walked over, pointed at the coffin and said, with a big smile, "You're next!"

What do you get if you cross the Hereford Town F.C. with an OXO cube?
A laughing stock.

Peter walked up to the sales lady in the clothing department of a large store in Gloucester.

"I would like to buy my wife a pretty pair of tights," he said. "Something cute with love-hearts or flower patterns."

"Oh, that's so sweet," exclaimed the sales lady, "I'll bet she'll be really surprised." "I'll say," said Peter, "she's expecting a new diamond ring!"

A policeman stops a drunk wandering the streets of Stroud at four in the morning and says, "Can you explain why you are out at this hour, sir?" The drunk replies, "If I was able to explain myself, I would have been home with the wife ages ago."

A man and his wife walked past a swanky new restaurant in Nailsworth. "Did you smell that food?" the woman asked. "Wonderful!"

Being the kind-hearted, generous man that he was, her husband thought, "What the hell, I'll treat her!"
So they walked past it a second time.

At a school in Tetbury, the maths teacher poses a question to little Josh, "If I give £500 to your dad on 12% interest per annum, what will I get back after two years."

"Nothing," says Josh.

"I am afraid you know nothing about maths, Josh," says the teacher crossly.

"I am afraid too, sir," replies Josh, "You don't know nothing about my father."

An expectant father rang the Stroud Maternity Hospital to see how his wife, who had gone into labour, was getting on. By mistake, he was connected to the county cricket ground.

"How's it going?" he asked.

"Fine," came the answer, "We've got three out and hope to have the rest out before lunch. The last one was a duck."

A man from Chipping Sodbury said to his wife, "Get your coat on love. I'm off to the club."

His wife said, "That's nice. You haven't taken me out for years." He said, "You're not coming with me...I'm turning the heating off when I go out."

Did you hear about the last wish of the henpecked husband of a house-proud wife?

He asked to have his ashes scattered on the carpet.

Have you heard about the latest machine in the arcade in Gloucester city centre?

You put ten pence in and ask it any question and it gives you a true answer. One visitor from Coventry tried it last week.

He asked the machine "Where is my father?" The machine replied: "Your father is fishing on the River Severn."

"Well," he thought, "That's daft for a start because my father is dead."

Next he asked, "Where is my mother's husband?"

The reply came back, "Your mother's husband is buried in Tewkesbury, but your father is still fishing on the River Severn."

A Brickhampton Golf Club player was going around the course talking to his caddy for the day between holes about an up and coming competition. "I've been drawn against Jack Smith from South Cerney, is he any good?"

The caddy checked for a moment and said, "He's absolutely rubbish. Can't get around the course with any ease. He set a new course record for the worst round ever that has only just been beaten."

"Oh, I should easily get through to the next round then, shan't I?" said the golfer complacently.

The caddy looked down at the scorecard and said, "I wouldn't bet on it!"

One freezing cold December day, two blondes went for a walk in the Forest of Dean in search of the perfect Christmas tree. Finally, after five hours looking, one turns to the other and says crossly, "That's it, I've had enough. I'm chopping down the next fir tree we see, whether it's decorated or not!"

Anne and Matt, a local couple, went to the Gloucestershire County Fair and found a weighing scale that tells your fortune and weight.

"Hey, listen to this," said Matt, showing his wife a small white card. "It says I'm bright, energetic, and a great husband."

"Yeah," Anna said, "And it has your weight wrong as well."

A new dentist set up a surgery in Painswick and quickly acquired a reputation for being a "Painless" dentist. But soon a local chap disputed this.

"He's a fake!" he told his mates. "He's not painless at all. When he stuck his finger in my mouth I bit him - and he yelled like anyone else."

A Hurrah Henry from Ledbury was driving around Cirencester in his fancy new car and realised that he was lost. The driver stopped a local character, old Tom, and said, "Hey, you there! Old man, what happens if I turn left here?"

"Don't know sir," replied Tom.

"Well, what if I turn right here - where will that take me?" continued the visitor.

"Don't know, sir," replied old Tom.

Becoming exasperated, the driver continued, "Well, what if I go straight on?"

A flicker of knowledge passed over old Tom's face but then he replied, "Don't know, sir."

"I say old man you don't know a lot do you?" retorted the posh bloke.

Old Tom looked at him and said, "I may not know a lot, sir, but I int lost like what you are!" With that, old Tom walked off leaving the motorist stranded.

Three sisters aged 92, 94 and 96 live in a house together in Avening. One night the 96 year-old draws a bath. She puts her foot in and pauses. She yells to the other sisters, "Were I getting in or out of the bath, my dear?"

The 94 year-old hollers back, "I don't know. I'll come up and see." She starts up the stairs but then she pauses, "Were I going upstairs or down?"

The 92 year-old is sitting at the kitchen table having tea listening to her sisters. She shakes her head and says, "I hope I never gets that forgetful, knock on wood." She raps on the oak table loudly. Then she shouts upstairs, "I'll come up and help the pair of you as soon as I see who's at the door."

A labourer in Stroud, shouted up to his roofer mate on top of an old terraced house, saying, "Don't start climbing down this ladder, Bert."

"Why not?" Bert called back.

"Cos I moved it five minutes ago!" replied his mate.

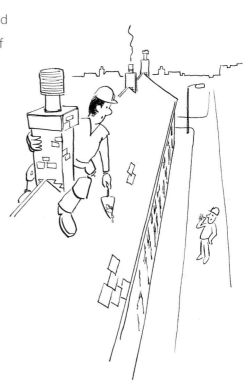

A bloke walked up to the foreman of a road laying gang in Gloucester and asked for a job. "I haven't got one for you today," said the foreman, looking up from his newspaper. "But if you walk half a mile down there, you'll find the gang and you can see if you like the work. I can put you on the list for tomorrow."

"That's great, mate," said the bloke as he wandered off down the road.

At the end of the shift, the man walked past the foreman and shouted, "Thanks, mate. See you in the morning."

The foreman looked up from his paper and called back, "You've enjoyed yourself then?"

"Yes, I have!" the bloke shouted, "But can I have a shovel or a pick to lean on like the rest of the gang tomorrow?"

An old chap from Upper Slaughter went to the G.P.

"Doctor," says the old boy, "There's summat up with me, I feel a bit under the weather, poorly."

"Flu?" asks the doc.

"No," says the old chap, "I rode here on me bike like I always does."

Patient: "Doctor, doctor! I've broken my arm in a couple of places!"
Doctor: "Then stay away from those places!"